MERCURY

The High-Speed Planet

by Ellen Lawrence

Consultants:

Suzy Gazlay, MA
Recipient, Presidential Award for Excellence in Science Teaching

Kevin Yates
Fellow of the Royal Astronomical Society

Editor: Mark J. Sachner
Designer: Emma Randall

Photo Credits:
NASA: Cover, 5 (bottom) 6, 8, 10, 11 (bottom), 12–13,
14–15, 16–17, 18–19, 20–21. Ruby Tuesday Books: 7, 9,
22. Science Photo Library: 4–5. Shutterstock: 11 (top).

Library of Congress Control Number: 2013939980

ISBN 978-1-909673-02-1

Printed and published in the United States of America

For further information including rights and
permissions requests, please contact our Customer
Service Department at 877-337-8577.

Contents

Words shown in **bold** in the text are explained in the glossary.

Welcome to Mercury

Imagine a world that is millions of miles from Earth.

In every direction, the land is rocky and covered with large holes called **craters**.

The Sun looks three times larger than it does from Earth.

During the day, it is so hot that some metals would melt.

At night, it is much colder than the coldest place on Earth.

Welcome to the **planet** Mercury!

A human could not visit Mercury because it is too hot in the daytime. Spacecraft have explored the planet, however, from just above its surface.

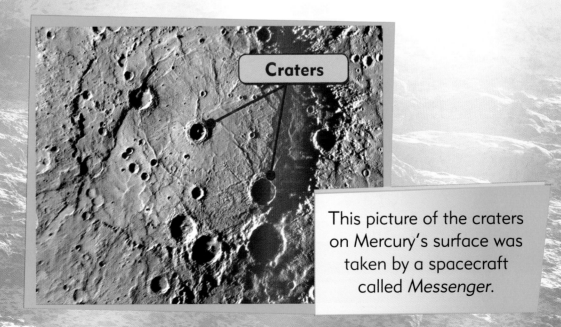

Craters

This picture of the craters on Mercury's surface was taken by a spacecraft called *Messenger*.

The Solar System

Mercury is moving through space at about 106,000 miles per hour (170,500 km/h).

It is moving around the Sun in an oval, or egg-shaped, path.

Mercury is one of eight planets circling the Sun.

The planets are called Mercury, Venus, our home planet Earth, Mars, Jupiter, Saturn, Uranus, and Neptune.

Icy **comets** and rocky **asteroids** are also moving around the Sun.

Together, the Sun, the planets, and other space objects are called the **solar system**.

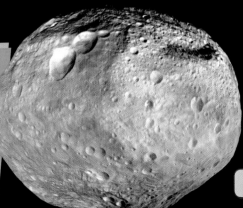

Asteroids are huge space rocks. Most of the asteroids circling the Sun are in a ring called the asteroid belt.

An asteroid

The Solar System
Mercury is the closest planet to the Sun.

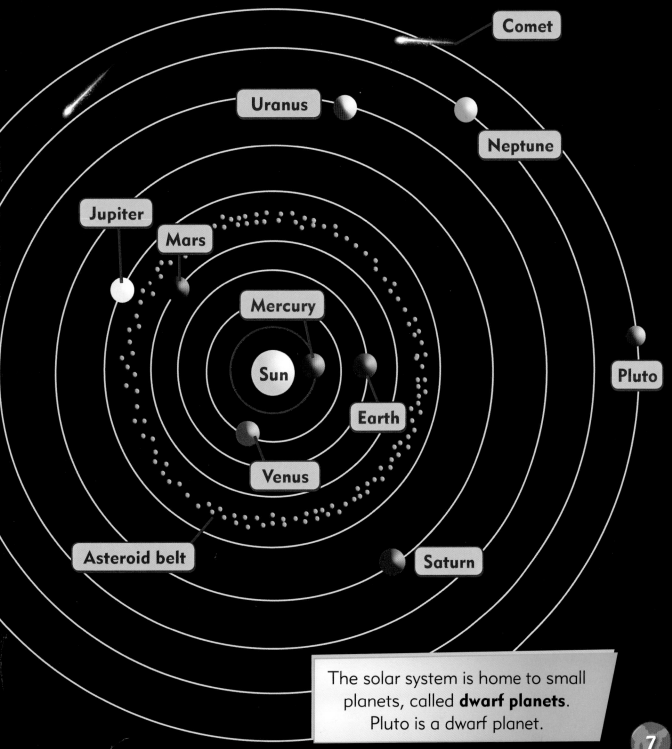

Comet

Uranus

Neptune

Jupiter

Mars

Mercury

Sun

Earth

Venus

Pluto

Asteroid belt

Saturn

The solar system is home to small planets, called **dwarf planets**. Pluto is a dwarf planet.

Mercury's Amazing Journey

The time it takes a planet to **orbit**, or circle, the Sun once is called its year.

Earth takes just over 365 days to orbit the Sun, so a year on Earth lasts 365 days.

Mercury is much closer to the Sun than Earth, so it makes a much shorter journey.

It takes Mercury about 88 Earth days to orbit the Sun.

This means that for every year on Earth, Mercury has about four years of its own!

As a planet orbits the Sun, it also spins, or **rotates**, like a top.

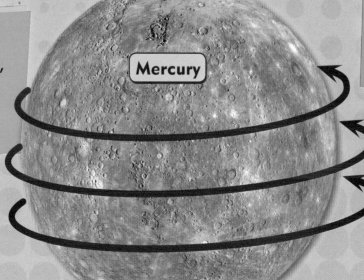

Mercury

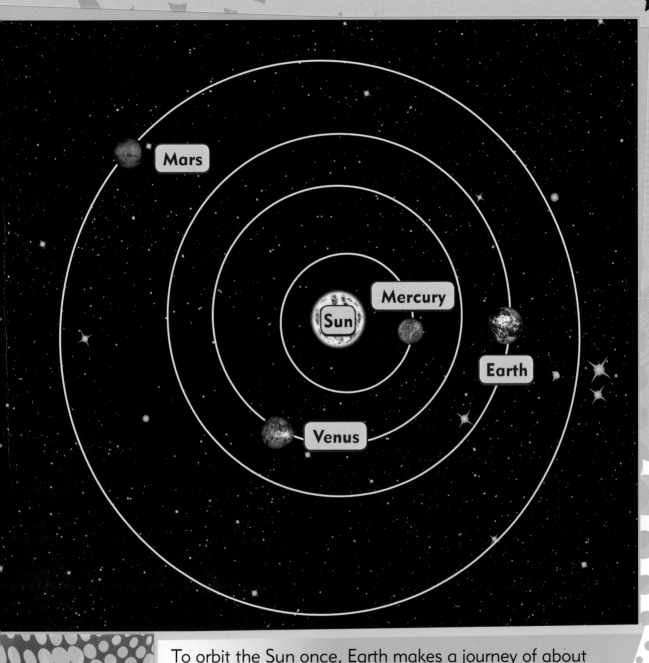

To orbit the Sun once, Earth makes a journey of about 584 million miles (940 million km). Mercury's journey is only about 224 million miles (360 million km).

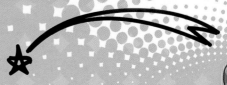

A Closer Look at ☆☆ Mercury

Mercury is the smallest planet in the solar system.

It is much smaller than Earth, and just slightly larger than Earth's Moon.

Our home planet, Earth, is covered with a thick layer of gases called an **atmosphere**.

It's these gases that make Earth's sky look blue.

Mercury does not have a thick atmosphere like Earth's.

So from Mercury the sky looks black whether it is day or night.

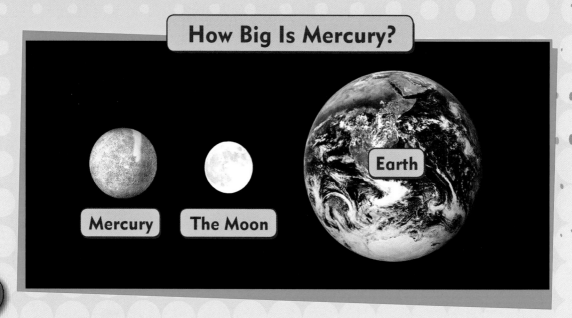

How Big Is Mercury?

Mercury   The Moon   Earth

A planet's atmosphere blocks some of the Sun's heat. Mercury has almost no atmosphere, and it is close to the Sun. That's why Mercury gets so hot in the daytime.

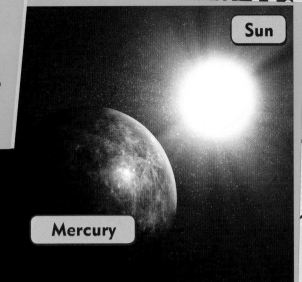

Sun

Mercury

Black sky

The surface of Mercury

At night, a planet's atmosphere traps some of the daytime heat. Mercury is super cold at night because all its heat escapes.

Small Planet, Huge Crater

The surface of Mercury is covered with craters.

These craters were made by asteroids, **meteoroids**, and comets that hit the planet's surface.

Mercury is also home to some truly giant craters called **impact basins.**

The planet's largest impact basin is about 930 miles (1,500 km) wide.

It's large enough that the entire state of Texas could fit inside!

When small rocky space objects hit a planet's atmosphere, they break apart or burn up. Mercury's very thin atmosphere cannot stop these rocks, so its surface gets hit again and again!

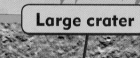

Large crater

Small craters inside the large crater

Mercury's gigantic impact
basin is called the Caloris
Basin (kuh-LOR-iss BAY-sin).
The large yellow area on this
picture of Mercury is
the Caloris Basin.

The Caloris Basin

Tiny Mercury, Giant Sun!

Every few years, Mercury can be seen from Earth as it passes in front of the Sun.

This movement across the Sun is called a **transit**.

As Mercury moves across the giant Sun, the planet looks like a tiny dot!

People should never look directly at the Sun because it will badly damage their eyes.

So scientists use special equipment to photograph a transit.

Then everyone can safely look at photos of this amazing event.

This photo shows Mercury passing in front of the Sun in November 2006.

The Sun

Sunspots

Mercury

The dark patches on the Sun are sunspots. Sunspots are areas that are cooler than the rest of the Sun's surface.

A Mission ☆ ☆ to Mercury

In August 2004, a rocket blasted off from Earth.

Aboard the rocket was a space **probe** called *Messenger*.

Messenger's mission was to travel to Mercury and study the planet.

It took six and a half years for *Messenger* to reach its destination.

In March 2011, the space probe began orbiting Mercury.

Rocket

Messenger blasts off from Cape Canaveral, Florida, in 2004, aboard a rocket.

Messenger

A crater on Mercury

Sunshade

This picture shows how *Messenger* might look orbiting Mercury. The space probe has a sunshade to protect it from the Sun's heat.

Amazing Discoveries

As it orbits Mercury, *Messenger* is sometimes only 120 miles (200 km) above the planet's surface.

During its mission, the space probe has made some amazing discoveries.

Messenger has taken photos of huge cliffs on the planet's surface.

It also discovered that there is ice on super-hot Mercury.

The ice is at the bottom of craters.

The craters are so deep that the Sun's heat and light never reach the ice!

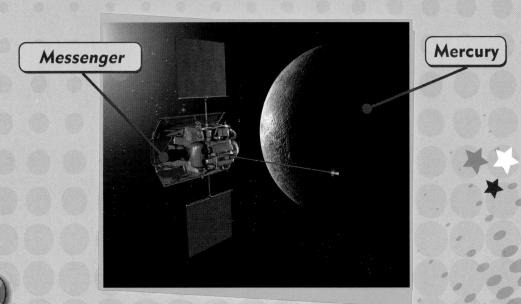

Messenger

Mercury

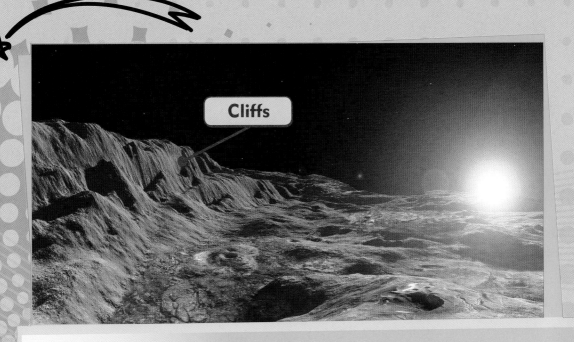

Cliffs

This picture was created on a computer using information from *Messenger*. It shows the giant cliffs on Mercury. The cliffs can be 1 mile (1.6 km) high and hundreds of miles long.

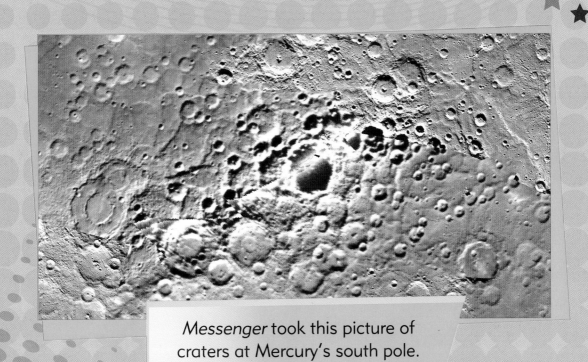

Messenger took this picture of craters at Mercury's south pole.

Mercury Fact File

Here are some key facts about Mercury,
the closest planet to the Sun.

Discovery of Mercury

Mercury can be seen in the sky without a telescope. People have known it was there since ancient times.

How Mercury got its name

The planet is named after Mercury, the ancient Romans' messenger of the gods.

Planet sizes

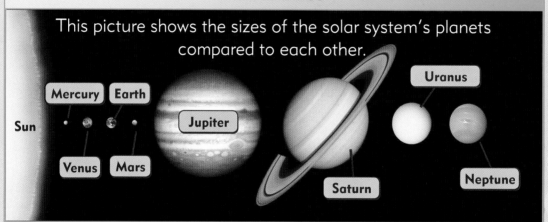

This picture shows the sizes of the solar system's planets compared to each other.

Mercury's size

3,032 miles (4,879 km) across

How long it takes for Mercury to rotate once

1,408 Earth hours

Mercury's distance from the Sun

The closest Mercury gets to the Sun is 28,583,702 miles (46,001,009 km).

The farthest Mercury gets from the Sun is 43,382,549 miles (69,817,445 km).

Length of Mercury's orbit around the Sun

223,679,248 miles (359,976,856 km)

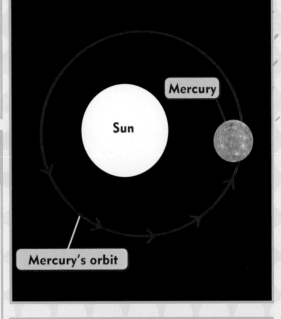

Mercury

Sun

Mercury's orbit

Average speed at which Mercury orbits the Sun

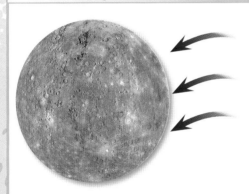

105,946 miles per hour (170,503 km/h)

Length of a year on Mercury

88 Earth days

Moons

Mercury has no moons.

Temperature on Mercury

Highest: 801°F (427°C)

Lowest: −279°F (−173°C)

Get Crafty
Crater Maker!

Rocky space objects hit the surface of Mercury and make craters. Using pebbles and plaster of Paris, you can make a model of Mercury's craters.

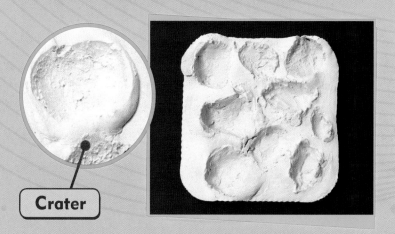

Crater

You will need:
- A bowl
- Plaster of Paris
- Water
- A spoon
- A foil pie tin
- Newspaper
- Pebbles or small pieces of rock

1. Put the plaster of Paris into the bowl. Add some water and stir until the mix looks like smooth pancake batter. Keep adding plaster or water until the mix is right. You will need enough mix to fill the pie tin.

2. Pour the mix into the pie tin and place the tin on the floor on top of some newspaper. Now, wait for the mix to start setting. Keep touching the mix with your finger. When it feels like ice-cream that is just getting soft, it's time to make craters!

Plaster mix

3. Drop a pebble into the pie tin. It will make a crater in the plaster mix! Quickly and carefully remove the pebble, then try again with a different pebble.

4. When the plaster mix is covered with craters, leave the plaster to set hard. This should take about 30 minutes. Then carefully remove your model from the pie tin.

Pebble

Glossary

asteroid (AS-teh-royd) A large rock that is orbiting the Sun. An asteroid can be as small as a car or bigger than a mountain.

atmosphere (AT-muh-sfeer) A layer of gases around a planet, moon, or star.

comet (KAH-mit) A space object made of ice, rock, and dust that is orbiting the Sun.

crater (KRAY-tur) A bowl-shaped hole in the ground. Craters are often caused by asteroids and other large, rocky objects hitting the surface of a planet or moon.

dwarf planet (DWARF PLAN-et) A round object in space that is orbiting the Sun. Dwarf planets are much smaller than the eight main planets.

impact basin (IM-pact BAY-sin) A very large crater that can be hundreds of miles wide.

meteoroid (MEE-tee-uh-royd) A small piece of rock or other material in space, usually one that has broken free from an asteroid or a comet.

orbit (OR-bit) To circle, or move around, another object.

planet (PLAN-et) A large object in space that is orbiting the Sun. Some planets, such as Mercury and Earth, are made of rock. Others, such as Jupiter, are made of gases and liquids.

probe (PROBE) A spacecraft that does not have any people aboard. Probes are usually sent to planets or other objects in space to take photographs and collect information. They are usually controlled by scientists on Earth.

rotate (ROH-tate) To spin around.

solar system (SOH-ler SIS-tem) The Sun and all the objects that orbit it, such as planets, their moons, asteroids, and comets.

transit (TRAN-zit) The passing of a small object in space across the face of a larger object. For example, the passing of Mercury across the face of the Sun is a transit of the Sun by Mercury.

Index

Read More

Hughes, Catherine D. *First Big Book of Space (National Geographic Little Kids).* Washington, D.C.: The National Geographic Society (2012).

James, Lincoln. *Mercury: The Iron Planet (Our Solar System).* New York: Gareth Stevens (2011).

Learn More Online

To learn more about Mercury, go to
www.rubytuesdaybooks.com/mercury